Student's Edition

Error Detection
Error Detection
Error Detection
Error Detection
Errer Detection
Error Detection
Error Detection
Error Ditection
Error Detection
Error Detection
Error Detection
Error Detection
Error Detection
Error Detecsiun
Error Detection
Error Detection
Error Detection

Exercises for the Instrumental Conductor
by Robert Spradling

CARL FISCHER®

Copyright © 2010 by Carl Fischer, LLC
International Copyright Secured.
All rights reserved including performing rights.
WARNING! This publication is protected by Copyright law. To photocopy or reproduce by
any method is an infringement of the Copyright law. Anyone who reproduces copyrighted
matter is subject to substantial penalties and assessments for each infringement.
Printed in the U.S.A.

JB93

ISBN 978-0-8258-7212-9

Table of Contents

Acknowledgements		5
Introduction		6
Bibliography		14
About Robert Spradling		14
American Overture	Joseph Willcox Jenkins	71
Augurs of Spring, The (from *The Rite of Spring*)	Igor Stravinsky, Arranged by Robert Spradling	73
Be Glad Then, America (Movement I from *New England Triptych*)	William Schuman	75
British Eighth	Zo Elliott	16
Canzona	Peter Mennin	77
Chester (Movement III from *New England Triptych*)	William Schuman	18
Chorale and Alleluia	Howard Hanson	38
Colonel Bogey (March)	Kenneth J. Alford, arr. Andrew Balent	19
Colonial Song	Percy Aldridge Grainger, ed. Timothy Topolewsky	80
Das neugeborne Kindelein (The Newborn Little Child)	Johann Sebastian Bach, arr. Robert Spradling	21
Du, o schönes Weltgebäude (You, O Wonderful Creator of the World)	Johann Sebastian Bach, arr. Robert Spradling	22
Early Light	Carolyn Bremer	82
Eine kleine Nachtmusik (Movement I), K. 525	Wolfgang Amadeus Mozart, arr. Andrew Balent	40
Elegy for a Young American	Ronald Lo Presti	84
Fairest of the Fair, The	John Philip Sousa, ed. Frederick Fennell	42
Fantasia in G Minor	Johann Sebastian Bach, ed. Richard Franko Goldman and Robert Leist	23
Folk Dances	Dmitri Shostakovich, arr. H. Robert Reynolds	24
Great Gate of Kiev, The (from *Pictures at an Exhibition*)	Modest Mussorgsky, arr. Larry Clark	26
Irish Tune from County Derry	Percy Aldridge Grainger, arr. Robert Spradling	44
Jubilee	George Kenny	27
Jupiter, the Bringer of Jollity (from *The Planets*)	Gustav Holst, arr. Andrew Balent	47
Kinetic Energy	Larry Clark	28
Meine Seele erhebet den Herrn (Glory Be to God the Father)	Johann Sebastian Bach, arr. Robert Spradling	30
Military Symphony in F (Movement I)	François Joseph Gossec ed. Richard Franko Goldman and Robert Leist	31
National Emblem	Edward Eugene Bagley, ed. Frederick Fennell	49
Pageant, Op. 59	Vincent Persichetti	51
Poet and Peasant Overture	Franz von Suppé, arr. by Henry Fillmore, ed. Robert Spradling	53
Prelude on an American Spiritual (*My Lord, What a Mornin'*)	Carl Strommen	55
Prelude (from *Prelude, Siciliano and Rondo*)	Malcolm Arnold, arr. John P. Paynter	57
Procession of the Nobles (from the Opera *Mlada*)	Nikolai Rimsky-Korsakov arr. Erik W. G. Leidzen, ed. Van B. Ragsdale	86
Quiet Song (Movement I from *Heart Songs*)	David Maslanka	33
Rondo (from *Prelude, Siciliano and Rondo*)	Malcolm Arnold, arr. John P. Paynter	59
Shepherd's Hey	Percy Aldridge Grainger, arr. Robert Spradling	88
Simple Gifts	American Folk Hymn, arr. Andrew Balent	34
St. Anthony's Divertimento	Franz Joseph Haydn, arr. Robert Spradling	61
Swan Lake (Theme from the Finale to Act II)	Peter Ilyich Tchaikovsky, arr. by Andrew Balent	35
Symphonic Overture	Charles Carter	62
Symphony for Band (Movement II)	Vincent Persichetti	89
Symphony No. 3 (Movement II)	Vittorio Giannini	64
Symphony No. 9 (*From the New World Symphony*, Finale)	Antonin Dvorak, trans. Erik W. G. Leidzen	91
Wallflower Waltz (from *Suite of Old American Dances*)	Robert Russell Bennett	66
Wer Nur Den Lieben Gott läßt walten (Whoever Lets Only the Dear God Reign)	Georg Neumark, arr. Robert Spradling	36
When Jesus Wept (Movement II from *New England Triptych*)	William Schuman	67

JB93

Contents by Level

Section 1: Introductory Exercises

British Eighth	Zo Elliott	16
Chester (Movement IIII from *New England Triptych*)	William Schuman	18
Colonel Bogey (March)	Kenneth J. Alford	19
Das neugeborne Kindelein (The Newborn Little Child)	Johann Sebastian Bach	21
Du, o schönes Weltgebäude (You, O Wonderful Creator of the World)	Johann Sebastian Bach	22
Fantasia in G Minor	Johann Sebastian Bach	23
Folk Dances	Dmitri Shostakovich	24
Great Gate of Kiev, The (from *Pictures at an Exhibition*)	Modest Mussorgsky	26
Jubilee	George Kenny	27
Kinetic Energy	Larry Clark	28
Meine Seele erhebet den Herrn (Glory Be to God the Father)	Johann Sebastian Bach	30
Military Symphony in F (Movement I)	François Joseph Gossec	31
Quiet Song (Movement I from *Heart Songs*)	David Maslanka	33
Simple Gifts	American Folk Hymn	34
Swan Lake (Theme from the Finale to Act II)	Peter Ilyich Tchaikovsky	35
Wer nur den lieben Gott läßt walten (Whoever Lets Only the Dear God Reign)	Georg Neumark	36

Section 2: Intlabelermediate Exercises

Chorale and Alleluia	Howard Hanson	38
Eine kleine Nachtmusik (Movement I), K. 525	Wolfgang Amadeus Mozart, Arranged by Andrew Balent	40
Fairest of the Fair, The	John Philip Sousa	42
Irish Tune from County Derry	Percy Aldridge Grainger	44
Jupiter, the Bringer of Jollity (from *The Planets*)	Gustav Holst	47
National Emblem	Edward Eugene Bagley	49
Pageant, Op. 59	Vincent Persichetti	51
Poet and Peasant Overture	Franz von Suppé	53
Prelude on an American Spiritual (*My Lord, What a Mornin'*)	Carl Strommen	55
Prelude (from *Prelude, Siciliano and Rondo*)	Malcolm Arnold	57
Rondo (from *Prelude, Siciliano and Rondo*)	Malcolm Arnold	59
St. Anthony's Divertimento	Franz Joseph Haydn	61
Symphonic Overture	Charles Carter	62
Symphony No. 3 (Movement II)	Vittorio Giannini	64
Wallflower Waltz (from *Suite of Old American Dances*)	Robert Russell Bennett	66
When Jesus Wept (Movement II from *New England Triptych*)	William Schuman	67

Section 3: Advanced Exercises

American Overture	Joseph Willcox Jenkins	71
Augurs of Spring, The (from the Ballet *The Rite of Spring*)	Igor Stravinsky	73
Be Glad Then, America (Movement I from *New England Triptych*)	William Schuman	75
Canzona	Peter Mennin	77
Colonial Song	Percy Aldridge Grainger	80
Early Light	Carolyn Bremer	82
Elegy for a Young American	Ronald Lo Presti	84
Procession of the Nobles (from the Opera *Mlada*)	Nikolai Rimsky-Korsakov	86
Shepherd's Hey	Percy Aldridge Grainger	88
Symphony for Band (Movement II)	Vincent Persichetti	89
Symphony No. 9 (*From the New World*, Finale)	Antonin Dvorak	91

JB93

Contents by Composer

Alford, Kenneth	Colonel Bogey (March)	19
Arnold, Malcolm	Prelude (from *Prelude, Siciliano and Rondo*)	57
	Rondo (from *Prelude, Siciliano and Rondo*)	59
Bach, Johann Sebastian	Das neugeborne Kindelein (The Newborn Little Child)	21
	Du, o schönes Weltgebäude (You, O Wonderful Creator of the World)	22
	Fantasia in G Minor	23
	Meine Seele erhebet den Herrn (Glory Be to God the Father)	30
Bagley, Edward Eugene	National Emblem	49
Balent, Andrew (Arranger)	Simple Gifts	34
Bennett, Robert Russell	Wallflower Waltz (from *Suite of Old American Dances*)	66
Bremer, Carolyn	Early Light	82
Carter, Charles	Symphonic Overture	62
Clark, Larry	Kinetic Energy	28
Dvorak, Antonin	Symphony No. 9 (*From the New World*, Finale)	91
Elliott, Zo	British Eighth	16
Giannini, Vittorio	Symphony No. 3 (Movement II)	64
Gossec, François Joseph	Military Symphony in F (Movement I)	31
Grainger, Percy Aldridge	Colonial Song	80
	Irish Tune from County Derry	44
	Shepherd's Hey	88
Hanson, Howard	Chorale and Alleluia	38
Haydn, Franz Joseph	St. Anthony's Divertimento	61
Holst, Gustav	Jupiter, the Bringer of Jollity (from *The Planets*)	47
Jenkins, Joseph Willcox	American Overture	71
Kenny, George	Jubilee	27
Lo Presti, Ronald	Elegy for a Young American	84
Maslanka, David	Quiet Song (Movement I from *Heart Songs*)	33
Mennin, Peter	Canzona	77
Mozart, Wolfgang Amadeus	Eine kleine Nachtmusik (Movement I), K. 525	40
Mussorgsky, Modest	Great Gate of Kiev, The (from *Pictures at an Exhibition*)	26
Neumark, Georg	Wer nur den lieben Gott läßt walten (Whoever Lets Only the Dear God Reign)	36
Persichetti, Vincent	Pageant, Op. 59	51
	Symphony for Band (Movement II)	89
Rimsky-Korsakov, Nikolai	Procession of the Nobles (from the Opera *Mlada*)	86
Schuman, William	Be Glad Then, America (Movement I from *New England Triptych*)	75
	Chester (Movement III from *New England Triptych*)	18
	When Jesus Wept (Movement II from *New England Triptych*)	67
Shostakovich, Dmitri	Folk Dances	24
Sousa, John Philip	Fairest of the Fair, The	42
Stravinsky, Igor	Augurs of Spring, The (from *The Rite of Spring*)	73
Strommen, Carl	Prelude on an American Spiritual (*My Lord, What a Mornin'*)	55
Suppé, Franz von	Poet and Peasant Overture	53
Tchaikovsky, Peter Ilyich	Swan Lake (Theme from the Finale to Act II)	35

Acknowledgements

It is impossible to thank everyone from whom I have learned over the years and who has made significant contributions to my development as a conductor and teacher. I have been fortunate to have so many great role models and friends who have unselfishly shared their knowledge and skills and who have helped me develop some understanding of the art and craft we call conducting.

I especially want to acknowledge Clifford K. Madsen, Chair for Music Education at The Florida State University, for teaching me the value of research and how to apply it to everyday situations. I would like to think that in some way his guidance and inspiration have touched my students. I would also like to thank my valued colleagues Craig Kirchhoff and Tim Diem at the University of Minnesota, Rod Winther and Terry Milligan at the Cincinnati College Conservatory of Music, Steve Steele at Illinois State University, and Bruce Moss and Carol Hayward at Bowling Green State University along with all of their students and mine at Western Michigan University for their invaluable help in the development of the error detection exercises. I especially want to recognize the brothers of the Mu Delta Chapter of Kappa Kappa Psi at Western, without whose help I would still be editing parts. In addition, I would like to thank my WMU colleagues, David Montgomery and John Lychner, for doing their jobs as well as mine in order for me to enjoy the luxury of a sabbatical leave to finish this workbook.

I am grateful to my former Syracuse University colleague and now Vice President and Editor-in-Chief at Carl Fischer Music, Larry Clark, for his enthusiastic support of this project and his insightful input throughout the publication process.

Finally, I want to thank my lovely wife, Diana, for her sharp editorial eyes, constant "cheerleading" and patience as so many other important things were placed on the "back burner" in order to make this workbook a reality.

—Robert Spradling

Introduction

Skills taught in today's conducting and instrumental methods classes include the selection of quality literature, researching and analysis of musical scores, an understanding of orchestration, the development of interpretation, the planning for rehearsals and performances, successful rehearsal techniques and the development of gesture in the conductor/ensemble interaction process to name a few.

The greatest limitation in most classes, and frustration to most conducting teachers, is the finite time that each student has to develop these skills on the podium in front of live musicians. This limited conducting time restricts development and one area in which this restriction is most evident is in the error-detection process.

In addition to the time spent in score preparation and in the development of well-defined gestures, the successful re-creation of the composer's intent requires the conductor to discern the differences between the printed page, with all appropriate interpretations, and the reality of what the ensemble is doing. Once again, limited time in class becomes an issue so that, more often than not, new conductors are left to develop this skill after they enter the field. The purpose of this workbook is to provide score excerpts at a variety of difficulty levels for conductors to use in the development of error-detection skills while striving to get appropriate musical results with live musicians.

Score Preparation

The key to all successful ensemble rehearsals and performances is preparation. Time invested by the conductor in the score and rehearsal preparation processes almost always pays off in more efficient, musically productive and ultimately satisfying rehearsals. There are a number of excellent resources for the study of score analysis techniques, so that topic will not be addressed in depth in this workbook. It is important to note, however, that the conductor's understanding of the composer, the stylistic characteristics of the period or time in which he or she wrote, influences upon the composer, and the fundamentals of score structure including form, meter(s), tempi, melodic, harmonic and rhythmic elements, phrasing, and expressive elements such as dynamics, articulation, blend, balance, and phrase direction are essential to establishing a musical model against which the conductor compares what is happening in reality from rehearsal to rehearsal. Score analysis is the foundation for all interpretation decisions made by the conductor. Poor musical decisions can usually be traced back to ineffective preparation.

The successful conductor learns to look at all of these elements and *anticipate* which of them in the score are potentially problematic. When potential problems are anticipated, potential solutions can be formed *a priori*, before they take place. If any of the anticipated problems are encountered in rehearsal, previously considered solutions are at the conductor's fingertips ready to be applied. If the anticipated problems don't occur, everybody wins! In either case, valuable time is saved, and musical results are achieved more efficiently.

What are some of the musical errors that can be anticipated by the conductor prior to rehearsal? The list is almost inexhaustible, but we can begin with some basic elements that will help to increase your aural perception skills.

Note Errors

If you consider "non-negotiable" elements such as meter, notes and rhythms as "objective" items, where the conductor really has no option other than what the composer has dictated, then determining whether or not these elements are being accurately performed *should* be relatively clear. The problem is, while some wrong notes (clams!) or rhythms are obvious and easy to identify, others fit in well with what is happening around them and, while incorrect, still sound pretty good. This is where the challenge comes for the conductor. Are those "objective," non-negotiable elements you *see* in the score in fact what you are hearing the ensemble play?

Key Signatures or Tonal Centers

A good place to begin is the key signature or tonal center, if one is evident. Any change of key signature within a composition is an automatic "red flag" for the conductor. You can anticipate that this may be a place to listen carefully for errors. Younger players in particular tend to miss the last flat or sharp in the key signature, particularly if the flat or sharp is *added or subtracted* to the key signature somewhere in the composition.

Accidentals

Accidentals present opportunities for conductors to anticipate errors. Accidentals may be used to alter melodic or harmonic elements in the score or, in some compositions, used throughout the score in place of a key signature. If a key signature is provided, the conductor should anticipate a change in tonality with accidentals and be prepared to react if the proper change does not take place. In scores without key signatures, the conductor must identify what kind(s) of tonalities the composer is presenting and at what points the accidentals change a previously established tonal center. Score analysis provides the information needed to anticipate potential errors.

Intervals and Direction

Conductors may anticipate errors by looking at individual parts for unusual interval leaps or musical sequences where intervals change in the midst of repeated rhythmic patterns. Attention to the direction of a musical line (ascending or descending) and any unusual or unexpected changes in direction can be a good place to anticipate note errors.

Rhythmic Errors

Rhythmic accuracy is the foundation of every musical score. If the rhythms in each part are not properly aligned, nothing else works! Incorrect rhythms are easily identified when all parts have the same rhythms at the same time. Since this rarely occurs beyond chorales, the conductor must look at rhythmic activity and study the relationships between different rhythms that happen at the same time. Sometimes these are fairly easy subdivisions but at other times can be somewhat complex requiring the conductor to find the lowest common subdivision and work out the relationship. A conductor can be relatively sure if it is a challenge for him/her to work out, it will be a good place to anticipate errors in the ensemble.

Syncopated and dotted rhythms are additional opportunities to anticipated errors, particularly among young players. Dotted eighth/sixteenth notes in particular are often performed as quarter- note/eighth- note triplet patterns. Compositions that have both triplet and dotted-eighth/sixteenth rhythms in them require the conductor to anticipate that the difference between the two rhythms may not be clearly audible. The secure, accurate performance of these rhythms will also tend to stabilize tempo.

Rhythmic complexity also tends to "mask" both note and expression errors. Remember to slow the tempo and isolate individual parts when necessary to hear the detail and clarify the problem(s). Younger players will need help internalizing the correct rhythm as the correction process is initiated. A system of verbal counting should be taught and incorporated into this process to teach correct rhythms and avoid repeated performance of incorrect rhythms.

Expression Errors

If we considered notes and rhythms as "non-negotiable" or "objective" elements, expressive elements might be considered "negotiable" or "subjective" in that they require interpretation and good musical judgment on the part of the conductor. Each ensemble has varying levels of experience among its members in addition to varying levels of technical and musical skills. In addition, not all ensembles are perfectly balanced in terms of instrumentation making it necessary for the conductor to adjust constantly individual or sectional performance to attain the overall musical goals outlined in the score as interpreted or realized by the conductor.

Dynamics

Dynamics are not "absolute" and are affected by many things including instrumentation balance, individual musicianship, ensemble maturity, and the conductor's expectations. Composers give direction in terms of dynamic levels and changes in these levels in anticipation of the conductor's ability to make the adjustments necessary in the ensemble for the listener to hear the indicated changes when and where indicated in the score and parts. This may mean having certain parts play out stronger or hold back a little in order to achieve the balance needed to achieve the ensemble's overall dynamic goals. Also, not all parts are necessarily going to have the same dynamics written for them at the same time. Recognizing dynamic differences in the score and anticipating how those differences will sound will help the conductor prepare for dynamic errors when they occur.

Places in the score where dynamic changes happen or where multiple dynamic levels occur simultaneously are "red-flag" areas where the conductor will want to pay attention. In many cases, the ensemble may either not accurately perform the indicated changes or they will do so unevenly and will need adjustment. With thorough score study, the conductor can anticipate those areas in the score where the potential for dynamic errors exist and prepare solutions.

Articulation

Articulation may be one of the most overlooked elements in the detection of musical errors and yet plays a most important role in the musical expression intended by the composer. While younger musicians often ignore articulation details, experienced musicians will perform articulation markings but not always to the extent that the conductor may want to hear them (another subjective decision). Therefore, it is important that the conductor carefully study each line in the score to see how the articulation markings complement or contrast those in the other lines. What distinction does the articulation marking bring to the musical line? What might the conductor anticipate as needing more or less emphasis to clarify the musical line? Do the articulations enhance or amplify dynamic changes or rhythmic activity?

The conductor must identify the range of articulation markings used by the composer and determine the length, weight, and stress of each in relation to others in the composition. A composer may use patterns or sequences of specific articulations over numerous measures or may use sudden abrupt articulation changes for impact or contrast. The conductor's responsibility is to identify what articulations the composer specifies, determine their musical function, and clarify them for the players.

Conductors may anticipate articulation problems by looking for places in the score where multiple types of articulations happen simultaneously. Other "red flags" might include *subito* changes in articulation patterns, articulation emphasis on "weak" beats or "off-beats", and articulation patterns that may not work easily with the rhythm patterns to which they are attached. Anticipate the need to clarify the difference between accents and staccatos in close proximity to each other. Look for articulations to be unclear where sudden dynamic changes take place.

Phrasing

As the conductor, you will determine the phrasing appropriate to each score and the phrase direction that results from your interpretation. Some composers are explicit in showing phrases while others are inconsistent or do not indicate them at all. It will be important for you to determine the function of the phases in each part and how they are shaped. Often, different parts will gain and lose intensity simultaneously adding emphasis to the musical line or direction. In other instances, musical lines may have differing functions and may change in intensity independently creating increased complexity to the musical direction. Regardless of the phrase shapes, it is important that the conductor recognize them as a part of the initial score preparation and provide appropriate information to the players in order to achieve the composer's intent.

Additional Considerations

Blend and Balance

Basic to the sound of an ensemble is the tone quality generated by each instrument and the blend and balance of that tone quality with other instruments in the ensemble. When considering blend, the conductor must evaluate the quality of the sound that results from the combination of two or more instruments playing the same musical line. If, for example, four clarinets share a musical line, the conductor will want to hear them blend so that they sound like one clarinet rather than four distinct individuals playing the same part. Similarly, if a musical line is shared by two or more different instruments, the conductor will want to blend them such that a new sound resulting from the combination or homogenization of the different instrumental tones results. Like mixing paint colors, the conductor may adjust the sound of each instrument to get the desired musical color or blend for that particular combination.

While blend is usually thought of as the careful integration of sounds on a single part, balance is the relationship between two or more parts. The conductor must, in the course of score study, determine what musical line or lines have prominence at any given time during the composition and see that the balance between all the lines being played allows the prominent line(s) to be heard. The balancing of the various musical lines in any composition is what brings clarity to the listener. Careful score study will enable the conductor to bring out melodies and countermelodies in relation to accompanying lines or know when an equal balance of all parts creates the specific sound or texture that the composer wants listeners to hear. Sometimes the composer helps this process with the designation of differing dynamic levels in the parts to more clearly expose the prominent line(s).

Many conductors begin the balancing of their ensembles with a concept known as the "pyramid of sound," fully explained by W. Francis McBeth in his book *The Effective Performance of Band Music*. This concept is based upon the technique of bringing out the lower voices in relation to the upper. For example, if a section, such as the clarinets or trumpets, is divided into three different parts, the second part would be played a little stronger than the first part, and the third part would be played a little stronger than the second. The first parts generally play in a higher tessitura than the second and third parts and are thus more prominent. Therefore, to balance the section, the lower parts must be brought out. In the same way, the lower-voiced sections in the ensemble must be balanced with the upper-voiced sections in order to achieve balance within the ensemble, what McBeth calls the "double pyramid." With this concept applied to all sections in the ensemble, a richer, more balanced quality of sound results and musical clarity is more easily achieved. In addition, intonation problems are dramatically reduced.

Intonation

Playing in tune was surely a challenge for the first two musicians who attempted to make music together and has been a challenge for ensembles and conductors ever since. Even though our standard of A=440 cycles per second was not universally adopted until 1936, ensembles have struggled to play in tune both vertically and horizontally throughout history. Like each of the previously identified musical properties where the potential for error exists, the topic of intonation requires much more space than is available in this workbook for in-depth consideration. There are, however, some initial concepts that are basic to the conductor's ability to identify and correct pitch errors. Key to solving pitch problems is the conductor's attention to the balance and blend issues addressed earlier. When ensemble members blend and balance their individual sounds so that they can hear all parts within their section, choir, and the full ensemble, discrepancies in pitch between instruments playing in unison or octaves and those playing different chord members can be more easily identified and corrected.

It is important to note that we humans tend to be more accepting of pitches that are sharp than we are of pitches that are flat. This explains why when we hear two instruments play the same pitch out of tune, we tend to adjust upward the one perceived to be flat even though it may actually be the one "in tune". We also tend to play the notes in an ascending line sharp while playing those in a descending line flat. Studies have shown that we often confuse intonation errors with poor tone quality and that this may become even more problematic depending upon the combination of instruments involved. The more we investigate the phenomenon of intonation, the more we find that many elements effect our perception of pitch. It is therefore important for the conductor to isolate perceived pitch problems and carefully determine the appropriate adjustments necessary to solve them.

An understanding of the overtone series as well as the tendencies of individual instruments to play particular notes sharp or flat is a good place for the conductor to begin. Encouraging players to sing pitches in tune and then match them with their instruments is a good tool for developing intonation security in the ensemble. Having the ensemble play a major chord based upon a pitch you would like to tune and leading them as they alternate between the major chord and the unison/octave pitch likewise helps the ensemble hear discrepancies and make accurate pitch adjustments. Having ensemble members tune to a low instrument such as the tuba or one that resonates a large number of overtones like the oboe, enables the musicians to better hear and compare their individual pitch to the sample. It is always a good technique for ensemble members to tune to the lowest part possible during the course of rehearsing or performing a composition. Tuning to artificially produced sounds as generated by mechanical tuners is not highly effective due to the lack of overtones produced by the tuner. It is a better technique to have the instrumentalist play a good sound with a centered pitch and then compare it to a tuner dial to see how sharp or flat the instrument may be on specific pitches after it is sufficiently warmed up. A conductor can help his/her ensemble members familiarize themselves with the pitch tendencies of their instruments by creating a form with a two- octave chromatic scale and a space next to each note to indicate the degree of sharpness or flatness for each note played. This can be done in teams with the player centering each pitch on his or her instrument and the partner checking the tuning device and marking down the degree of pitch variation on the form. The partners may then trade responsibilities and in the end, each will have an indication of the pitch tendencies for their instruments. This process may be done at various points in time to see how each instrumentalist is progressing in the anticipation of pitch variance and in their ability to make the adjustments necessary to better play in tune.

Conductors throughout history have developed effective strategies for isolating and correcting pitch problems in their ensembles and with a little research, you will be able to find many successful approaches that will help your ensemble play better in tune. Your instructor will be helpful in pointing you in the right direction as you begin your search.

Strategies

Many errors are immediately obvious to the conductor while others may be "sensed" if not immediately identified. Pinpointing discrepancies between the written score and the ensemble's sound and correcting them as efficiently as possible is the goal of every conductor. Part of the process is recognizing limitations to what we can perceive and identify at any given time.

With experience and practice, our abilities to accurately perceive multiple parts improve. Accurately monitoring two different parts is not overly difficult, while critiquing three or more simultaneously becomes increasingly more challenging. Recognizing this, it is important for the conductor to develop a strategy that isolates parts where errors are recognized or "sensed" rather than attempting to pinpoint them while the entire ensemble plays.

In general, the outside, or highest and lowest, parts are the easiest to hear making the errors in them more obvious. An inside part, however, may need to be isolated individually or in combination with one other part in order to clarify what is happening. Errors are often discovered when isolating parts in an attempt to improve musicality. While incorrect notes and rhythms (the objective elements) are easier to identify, the expressive (subjective) elements may be more illusive and only become clearer as you isolate individual parts.

A conductor can think of the rehearsal process as a mechanic might view rebuilding a motor. If the motor is not running smoothly, the mechanic attempts to isolate parts that may not be functioning properly. In many cases, more than one part contributes to the problem, so areas of the motor are disassembled, parts fixed, reassembled and tested. Just as the mechanic's knowledge of the motor helps him anticipate problems and pinpoint parts to observe, so does the conductor's knowledge of the score provide the foundation for the anticipation and isolation of errors that interfere with the composer's musical intent.

One sure technique that most good conductors use for error detection and correction is to slow the tempo to a point that isolated lines may be clearly perceived and problems identified. Once errors are corrected, the tempo may be gradually increased while maintaining accurate, musical performance.

Over time, conductors develop an additional skill that is also useful in an efficient rehearsal. This skill involves recognizing "mistakes of the moment" as opposed to mistakes of concept. Mistakes of concept are errors the players do not realize they are making. The wrong notes, rhythms and expressive elements (or lack thereof!) that are repeatedly performed are those the conductor must identify and correct. If the players understood they were playing errors, they would not do so. The conductor's job is to clarify the player's understanding. For the musical excerpts in this workbook, errors are included in the players' parts. They will be playing what they see and will not know, in many instances, that it is different from what the score indicates.

In contrast, there is the "mistake of the moment." When the error is performed, the conductor looks at the player(s) only to see eyes roll, a look of disgust or embarrassment, and perhaps a part marked indicating the mistake has been recognized. A simple confirmation or quick review may be all that is necessary.

Process

There are many ways to run a successful rehearsal and you will, over time, develop the techniques that work best for you. Your instructor will have suggestions that will add to your effectiveness. One technique that is common to most successful conductors is the establishment of a positive working environment. Research has shown that conductors who identify and reinforce *correct* musical responses are more time efficient in rehearsals. Likewise, conductors who identify errors *without negative comments*, offer solutions, and positively reinforce correct responses have more successful and time-efficient rehearsals.

To be effective in the correction of errors, it is important to follow a simple process that generally clarifies the "who, where, what and how" of the process. First, when it is necessary to stop the music-making process, identify the part or parts that you wish to address. Second, identify the measure(s) and beat(s) requiring attention. Third, identify the element(s) in question and give instruction as to what you should be hearing. An example might be, "Clarinets; in measure 77, beat 3, my score indicates a D♭ on your part. Is that correct? Good, then let's play that measure to be sure we are all doing it correctly."

At this point, if they all perform it correctly, you should reinforce their understanding by saying something like, "That's it, thank you. Let's keep going." If one or more misses the note again, you may follow up with something like, "We still have a difference of opinion on beat 3. Double check that you have a D♭ and let's try it one more time." Continued errors will indicate a lack of recognition on the part of the player(s) or possibly, in the case of younger players, not knowing how to finger the D♭. Regardless, a positive, patient approach to correcting the problem will pay dividends in terms of the players' error correction and their attitude toward the music and the process as the problem is resolved. Helping players correct errors without them becoming defensive about their performance will likewise produce better musical results and maintain a positive environment.

While most transposed scores give the conductor the benefit of seeing exactly what the players see on their parts, condensed or non-transposed scores do not. The conductor must recognize when a score is not transposed and be prepared to converse with players in terms of the notes they are reading *on their parts* and not confuse the issues by expecting the players to do the transposition. Rather than asking, for example, the alto saxophone players if, in measure 41, beat 2, they have a concert E♭ as is indicated in your non-transposed score, you should ask them if they have a C. Conductors, not players should do the transposing in rehearsal. All score excerpts in this workbook are non-transposed (or concert pitch) while the players' parts are transposed. This will give you as the conductor the opportunity to practice your transposition while interacting with the ensemble members.

Conducting the Music

The task of error detection may, at first, feel like spinning a lot of plates at one time, and in a sense, you are. The most important issue in the process is that you continue to be a *musical* leader. Your musical decisions, your instructions, your non-verbal communication with the ensemble, and your representation of the composer in communicating to the audience the intent of the music are primary in your rehearsal/performance process. You are always a part of the ensemble, never a separate entity. The generation of wonderful music comes from the conductor's commitment to the score and ability to coordinate the musical output of the various ensemble members.

In order to be a musical leader, you must develop the ability to recognize those things you hear that do not match what is in the score or what you expect to hear as a result of your score study. With experience, many errors will become "distractions" from what you expect to hear and easily identified. Other errors will me more subtle and found as your rehearsal process exposes them. You must never abandon your efforts to communicate musical intent and direction while on the podium regardless of the problems you encounter.

Instructions for Conductors

Establish an error identification/correction process of: 1) identifying the part(s) in question; 2) identifying the measure(s) and beat(s) in question; 3) providing the correct musical element for the players; 4) allowing them to respond and perform the musical element correctly. Positively reinforce accurate performance or reinstruct.

When correcting errors, address every transposing instrument as the *written pitch* that occurs in their parts, not the concert pitch that is shown in your score. **Note:** There are occasional octave transpositions in the parts to accommodate instrument ranges. These are not considered errors.

Sometimes, more than one error can happen simultaneously or the same error might occur in more than one part. This is not to "trick" you, but to open your ears to a natural occurrence.

Instructions for Performers

Attend to and perform *every detail* (especially expression) as indicated on your parts, even if it goes against your best musical instincts! Your part may include indications that are opposed to what you are hearing in other parts and what you are doing may also be contrary to the conductor's gestures. These may in fact be the errors the conductor must correct.

Do not offer help to the conductor by asking questions relative to "suspected" errors in your part. This may remove an opportunity for the conductor to find and correct errors in your part.

Similar errors *may* occur in more than one part. If an error is identified in another part and also exists in your part though has not been identified by the conductor, do not make the change and continue to play as written until corrected.

Bibliography

Geringer, J.M. and C.K. Madsen. "Verbal and Operant Discrimination-Preference for Tone Quality and Intonation." *Psychology of Music,* 1981, 9, (1), 26–30.

Greer, R.D. "The Effect of Timbre on Brass-wind Intonation." *Experimental Research in Music: Studies in the Psychology of Music,* 1970, 6, 65–94.

Madsen, Clifford K., R. Douglas Greer, and Charles H. Madsen, Jr., eds. *Research in Music Behavior: Modifying Music Behavior in the Classroom.* New York: Teachers College Press, Columbia University, 1975.

Madsen, C.K. and J.M. Geringer. "Preference for Trumpet Tone Quality versus Intonation." *Council for Research in Music Education,* 1976, 46, 13–22.

McBeth, W. Francis. *Effective Performance of Band Music.* San Antonio: Southern Music Company, 1972.

Spradling, Robert L. "Perception and Preference of Tone Quality/Intonation Variables in Flute/Oboe Duets by Woodwind/Brass Performers." *Journal of Band Research,* Spring, 1985

———. "The Effect of Time-out from Performance on Attentiveness and Attitude of University Band Students." *Journal of Research in Music Education,* Summer, 1985.

About Robert Spradling

Robert Spradling has over forty years of experience as a music educator and instrumental conductor. During that time he has taught conducting at the undergraduate and graduate levels while contributing to in-service conducting clinics and workshops. He has maintained an active schedule as clinician and guest conductor, while his research interests have centered upon conductor/ensemble interaction. His experience includes teaching in middle- and high-school bands in the state of Florida, as well as tenures as Director of Bands at Syracuse University and Western Michigan University.

Error Detection Exercises for the Instrumental Conductor evolved out of exercises Dr. Spradling developed for his own conducting classes and workshops and has shown to have a positive impact upon his students' aural skills and awareness while on the conducting podium.

Section 1:
Introductory Exercises

British Eighth

ZO ELLIOTT
(1891–1964)

Chester
(Movement III from *New England Triptych*)

WILLIAM SCHUMAN
(1910–1992)

Copyright © 1957 by Merion Music Inc. Theoder Presser Co. Sole Representative.
Copyright Renewed. All Rights Reserved.
International Copyright Secured. Printed in the U.S.A.
Unauthorized copying, arranging, or recording is an infringement of copyright. Infringers are liable under the law.

JB93

Colonel Bogey
(March)

KENNETH J. ALFORD
Arranged by Andrew Balent

Das neugeborne Kindelein
(The Newborn Little Child)

JOHANN SEBASTIAN BACH
(1685–1750)
Arranged by Robert Spradling

Du, o schönes Weltgebäude
(You, O Wonderful Creator of the World)

JOHANN SEBASTIAN BACH
(1685–1750)
Arranged by Robert Spradling

Copyright © 2010 by Carl Fischer, LLC.
International Copyright Secured.
All rights reserved including performing rights.

Fantasia in G Minor

JOHANN SEBASTIAN BACH
(1685–1750)
Arranged by Robert Spradling

Copyright © 2010 by Carl Fischer, LLC.
International Copyright Secured.
All rights reserved including performing rights.

Folk Dances

DMITRI SHOSTAKOVICH
(1906–1975)
Arranged by H. Robert Reynolds

The Great Gate of Kiev
from *Pictures at an Exhibition*

MODEST MUSSORGSKY
(1839–1881)
Arranged by Larry Clark

Jubilee

GEORGE KENNY

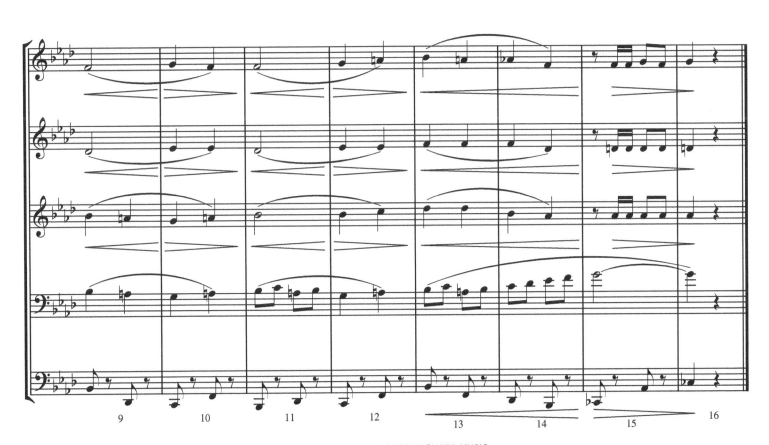

Kinetic Energy

LARRY CLARK
(b. 1963)

Meine Seele erhebet den Herrn
(Glory Be to God the Father)

JOHANN SEBASTIAN BACH
(1685–1750)
Arranged by Robert Spradling

Moderato (♩ = 92)

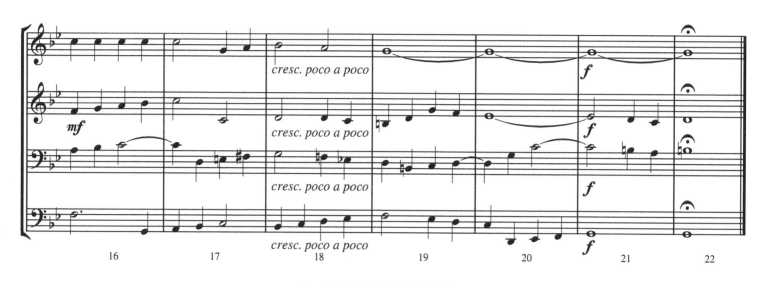

Copyright © 2010 by Carl Fischer LLC.
International Copyright Secured.
All rights reserved including performing rights.

Military Symphony in F
(Movement I)

FRANÇOIS-JOSEPH GOSSEC
(1734–1809)
Edited by Richard Franko Goldman
and Robert Leist

Allegro maestoso

Copyright © 1950 by Mercury Music Corp. Theodore Presser co. Sole Representative.
Copyright Renewed. All Rights Reserved.
International Copyright Secured. Printed in the U.S.A.
Unauthorized copying, arranging, or recording is an infringement of copyright. Infringers are liable under the law.

Quiet Song
Movement I from *Heart Songs*

DAVID MASLANKA
(b. 1943)

Simple Gifts

American Folk Hymn
Arranged by Andrew Balent

Copyright © 1986 by Carl Fischer Inc.
All Rights Assigned to Carl Fischer LLC.
International Copyright Secured. All rights reserved including performing rights.

35

Swan Lake
(Theme from the Finale to Act II)

PETER ILYICH TCHAIKOVSKY
(1840–1893)
Arranged by Andrew Balent

Copyright © 2001 by Carl Fischer LLC.
International Copyright Secured.
All rights reserved including performing rights.

JB93

Wer nur den lieben Gott läßt walten
(Whoever Lets Only the Dear God Reign)

GEORG NEUMARK
(1621–1681)
Arranged by Robert Spradling

Copyright © 2010 by Carl Fischer LLC.
International Copyright Secured.
All rights reserved including performing rights.

Section 2:
Intermediate Exercises

Chorale and Alleluia

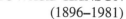
HOWARD HANSON
(1896–1981)

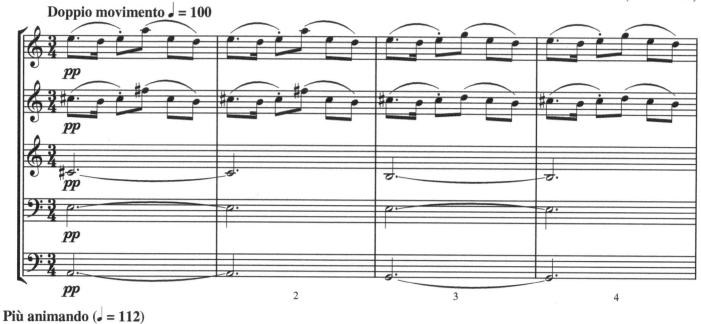

Eine kleine Nachtmusik
(Movement I)

WOLFGANG AMADEUS MOZART, K. 525
(1756–1791)
Arranged by Andrew Balent

Copyright © 1996 by Carl Fischer Inc.
All Rights Assigned to Carl Fischer LLC.
International Copyright Secured. All rights reserved including performing rights.

JB93

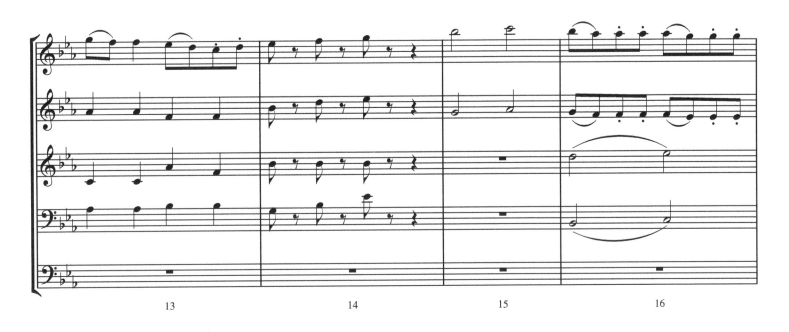

The Fairest of the Fair

JOHN PHILIP SOUSA
(1854–1932)
Edited by Frederick Fennell

Irish Tune from County Derry

PERCY ALDRIDGE GRAINGER
(1882–1961)
Arranged by Robert Spradling

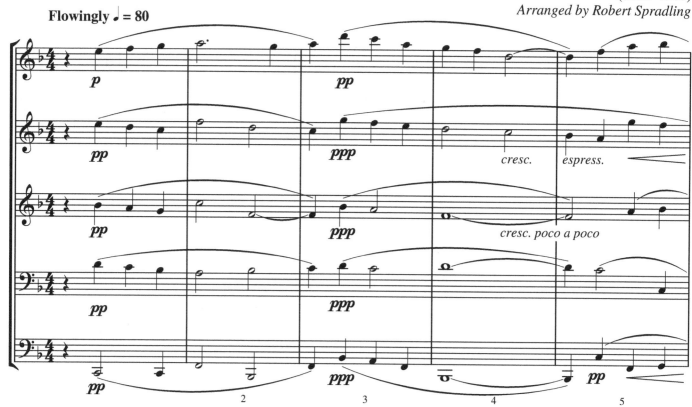

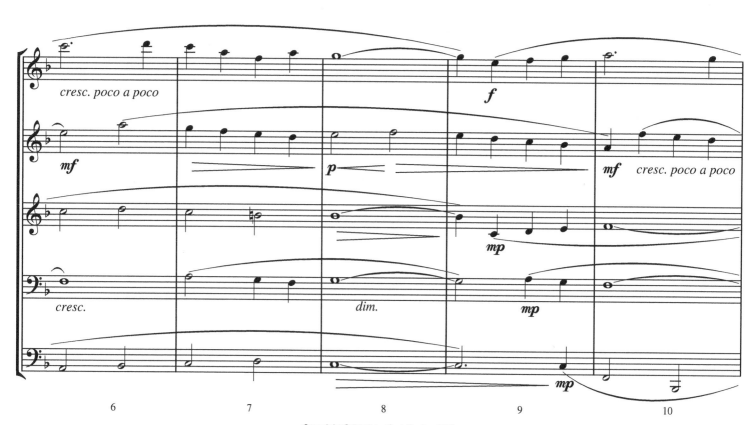

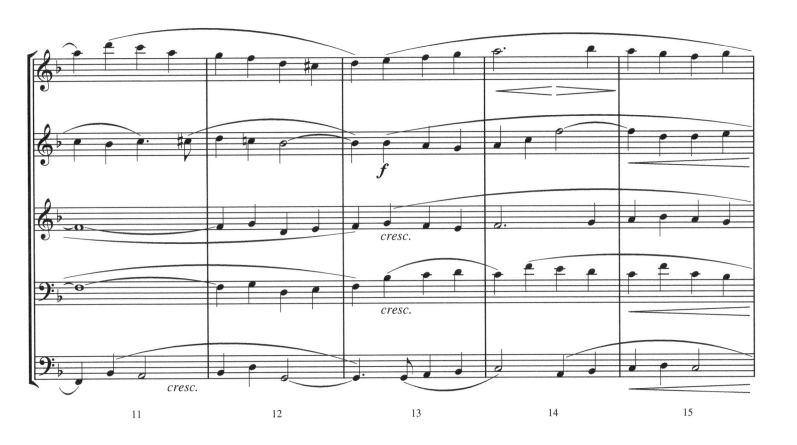
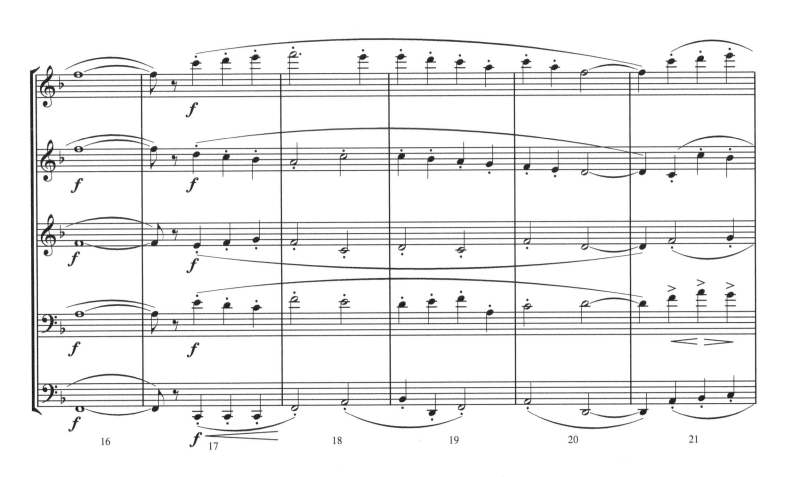

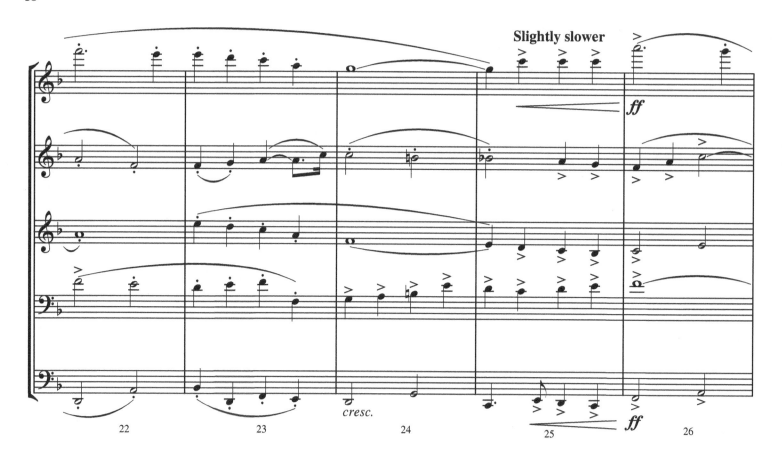

Jupiter, the Bringer of Jollity
from *The Planets*

GUSTAV HOLST
(1874–1934)
Arranged by Andrew Balent

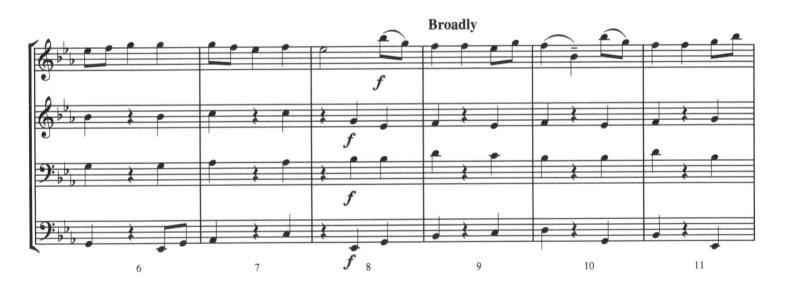

Copyright © 1999 by Carl Fischer LLC.
International Copyright Secured.
All rights reserved including performing rights.

48

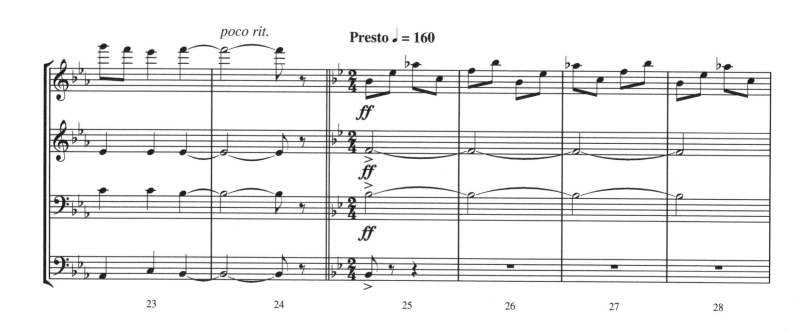

JB93

National Emblem

EDWIN EUGENE BAGLEY
(1857–1922)
Edited by Frederick Fennell

Pageant

VINCENT PERSICHETTI, Op. 59
(1915–1987)

Poet and Peasant Overture

FRANZ von SUPPÉ
(1819–1895)
Arranged by Henry Fillmore
Edited by Robert Spradling

54

Prelude on an American Spiritual
(*My Lord, What a Mornin'*)

CARL STROMMEN

Prelude
from *Prelude, Siciliano and Rondo*

MALCOLM ARNOLD
(1921–2006)
Arranged by John P. Paynter

59

Rondo
from *Prelude, Siciliano and Rondo*

MALCOLM ARNOLD
(1921–2006)
Arranged by John P. Paynter

Copyright © 1979 by PATERSON'S Publications, Ltd.
Exclusively distributed by Carl Fischer, LLC.
International Copyright Secured. All rights reserved including performing rights.

St. Anthony's Divertimento

FRANZ JOSEPH HAYDN
(1732–1809)
Arranged by Robert Spradling

Symphonic Overture

CHARLES CARTER
(1926–1999)

Symphony No. 3
(Movement II)

VITTORIO GIANNINI
(1903–1966)

Wallflower Waltz
from *Suite of Old American Dances*

ROBERT RUSSELL BENNETT
(1894–1981)

When Jesus Wept
(Movement II from *New England Triptych*)

WILLIAM SCHUMAN
(1910–1992)

Section 3:
Advanced Exercises

American Overture

JOSEPH WILLCOX JENKINS
(b. 1928)

Copyright © 1955, 1956, 2003 by Theoder Presser Co., King of Prussia, PA.
All Rights Reserved. *International Copyright Secured.* Printed in the U.S.A.

JB93

The Augurs of Spring
from the Ballet *The Rite of Spring*

IGOR STRAVINSKY
(1882–1971)
Arranged by Robert Spradling

74

Be Glad Then, America
(Movement I from *New England Triptych*)

WILLIAM SCHUMAN
(1910–1992)

Copyright © 1957 and 1975 by Merion Music Inc. Theoder Presser co. Sole Representative.
Copyright Renewed. All Rights Reserved.
International Copyright Secured. Printed in the U.S.A.

Canzona

PETER MENNIN
(1923–1983)

Colonial Song

PERCY ALDRIDGE GRAINGER
(1882–1961)
Edited by Timothy Topolewski

JB93

Copyright © 2001 by Carl Fischer LLC.
International Copyright Secured

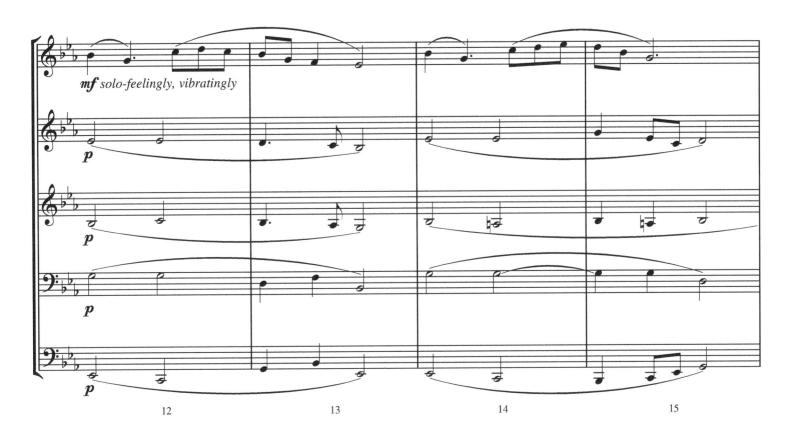

Early Light

CAROLYN BREMER

Elegy for a Young American

RONALD LO PRESTI
(b. 1933)

Procession of the Nobles
from the Opera *Mlada*

NIKOLAI RIMSKY-KORSAKOV
(1844–1908)
Arranged by Erik W.G. Leidzén
Edited by Van B. Ragsdale

Copyright © 1999 by Carl Fischer LLC.
International Copyright Secured. All rights reserved including performing rights.

Shepherd's Hey

PERCY ALDRIDGE GRAINGER
(1882–1961)
Arranted by Robert Spradling

Symphony for Band
(Movement II)

VINCENT PERSICHETTI
(1915–1987)

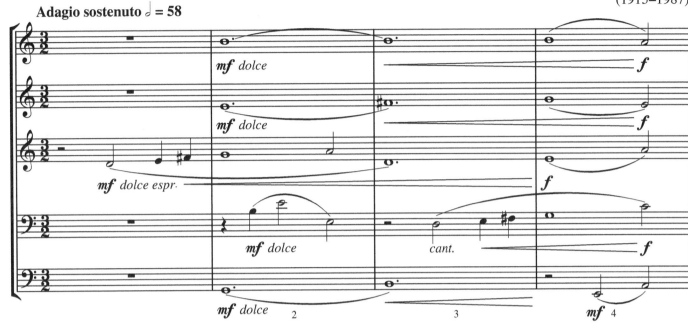

Copyright © 1958 by Elkan-Vogel, Inc.
Copyright Renewed. All Rights Reserved.
International Copyright Secured. Printed in the U.S.A.

Symphony No. 9
(From the New World)
(Finale)

ANTONIN DVORAK
(1841–1904)
Transcribed by Erik W.G. Leidzén

Copyright © 1936 by Carl Fischer Inc.
All Rights Assigned to Carl Fischer LLC.
International Copyright Secured. All rights reserved including performing rights.